THE ZODIAC

END OF THE GAME

Aleksandar Kulauzov

ISBN

Hardcover: 979-8-90190-414-5

Paperback: 979-8-90190-413-8

Book Publishing Group LLC

42 Broadway 12th floor, New York, NY 10004

www.bookpublishinggroupllc.com

About the Author

Aleksandar Kulauzov is a Serbian armchair detective and a code breaker, born in Yugoslavia. The author of two books about the Zodiac, an American serial killer who operated in the 1960's and 1970s, played a game of clues. In this book, Aleksandar presented the way to find the Zodiac's own words: "This is the way cipher is."

The Zodiac
"Memory of The Killer"

It's 1975, San Francisco, California. The end game is the Zodiac serial killer; the police are wondering if he has finally stopped? By this point, solving this case became "The ego game," as the San Francisco police admitted. Who will be the one to solve the case, rather than who is really the Zodiac?

The last confirmed Zodiac murder took place in downtown San Francisco, during the late evening hours of October 11, 1969. On what should've been a night like countless others, the taxi driver, Paul Stine, was executed once he reached his requested destination, shot by the passenger in the back seat. It was the Zodiac. Through his letters mailed to the press, the Zodiac confirmed it was him by sending his own sample of Stine's blood-stained shirt, a piece of bloody fabric included in the envelope mailed on October 13, 1969.

Clearly, The Zodiac was playing with the police; for him, the game was on. The letters would keep showing up in the press, reaching the police and eventually the public. Some letters would include ciphers that might reveal his full identity, as he claimed. Some ciphers were long, some short. Some were deciphered, some not…

On April 20, 1970, the Zodiac mailed what's now known as a Z13 cipher. My name is ⌐, followed by a 13-character cipher, the code that hasn't been solved until now.

In November 2024, I was able to tap into the memory of the killer, crack the code, and come up with the full identity of the person responsible for the

Zodiac crimes. In the world of symbols, the 55-Year-Old Mystery is finally revealed!

Z13 Cipher
"Catch Me If You Can"

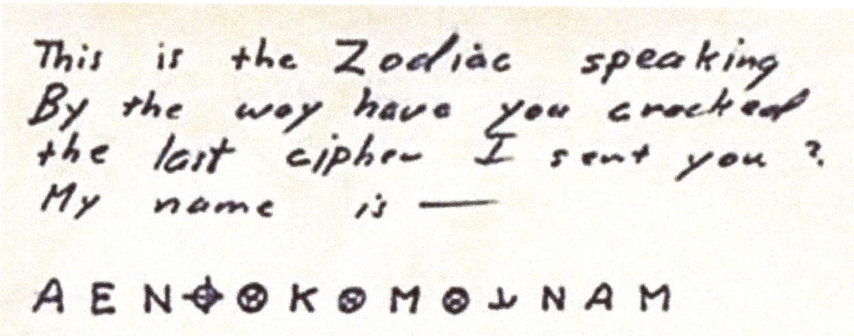

Above is the portion of the Z13 letter, a small introduction message followed by the cipher. Normally, the first thing you would do is take a good look at the 13-character cipher, but that's not what we are going to do here. What I did was look at the message above and see if anything stood out. What stood out are these 2 words, "last" and "name", just notice how they are visibly separated from the rest of the sentence, which then becomes a thing on its own "last name" – easily fits together, then it reads: "The last name cipher…" or "My last name is…" Followed by this line "⌐", which could simply mean "line" or just "dash", but quick note here, if we go into his mind we know he does not want to get caught, he is really going to do his best to hide his name, yet he wants to somehow provide his name to the authorities and get that pleasure from still remaining unidentified after all. "Catch me if you can."

So, if you carefully notice, the line is slightly going upwards, which then becomes a symbol for "incline." If I apply the word incline in place of the "⌐" symbol, then it would begin to read: "The last name cipher is incline" or "My last name is in cline", the last name is in this word "Cline".

That seems to flow well, so for now I'm going to write down:

"My Last Name Is Cline"

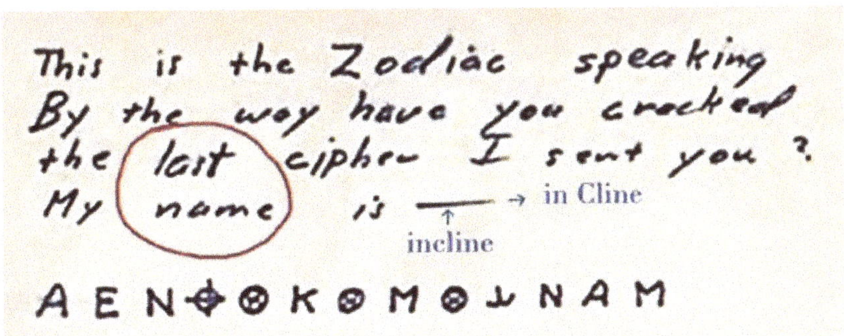

The next step is to move on to these 13 characters. You might think here, if we already have the last name, what's the point of moving on? We'll see how all this fits together. At first glance, "A E N" means really nothing significant, then we have the Zodiac sign ⚹, that's him while murdering, as he himself made that clear, it's his signature in his writings, that we know for sure. Next is this circled 8 "⑧." Which really struck me as the 8-ball in the pool game, and we know in his letters he does mention the billiard game, a game where the 8-ball is the end game. In order to win the game, you need to sink the 8-ball. That's the goal of the game. In The

Zodiac's mind, this is all a game he is presenting, a game where the goal is finding him, finding his name. The Zodiac is the endgame, so "⑧" is him as well. This time there are 3 of him surrounding "K" and "M", which does seem to indicate that those 2 letters could be something important. Maybe his initials or something close to it. Here, he could be saying that there are 3 people murdering as the Zodiac, or maybe his 3 names fit into one persona. In other words, he might have 3 names, or 3 last names, as we established that this might very well be the last name cipher.

If we add all that together into one number, we get 3 x 8 = 24. Given the period of the crimes, this could easily be his year of birth, so I'm going to write down 1924 for now, and see how that plays out.

1924

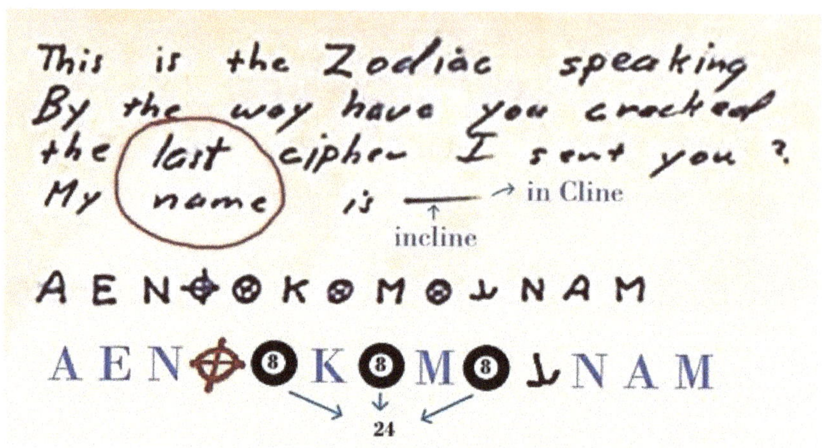

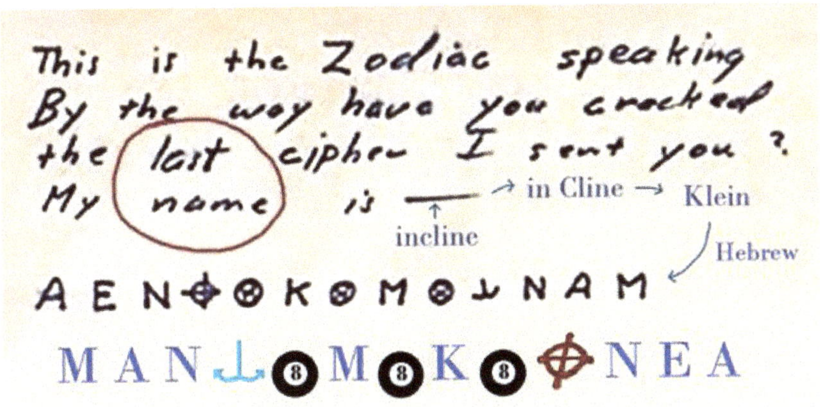

We are now back at the Navy sign, coming into "M" and "K", surrounded by 3 "⑧'s." On one side, there is the Navy symbol, on the other side, we see his Zodiac sign attached to the other ⑧. As if he wants to inform us that one ⑧, or one last name, is associated with him in the Navy, another ⑧ is him as The Zodiac. The M could really stand for his first name, but there is no way for us to know what it could be exactly, so if I just write:

Navy M K

Or as it reads:

Navy eM Kay

After reading this line number of times, it sure sounds like: "Navy am Kay" as if he wants to say:

In the Navy, I am Kay

This "M" can also be linked to the capital "M" in the "My name is" line. In some way, M is pointing down towards the "M" in the cipher, which could be some kind of indication that these 2 Ms are associated. Even with that interpretation, we get the same solution, instead of "I aM", it would go on to read "My name is KLEIN, My name is KAY…"

At this point, we cannot ignore these 3 ⑧'s, again the 8-ball is the endgame. In his mind, he is the endgame. And now that we also have Kay as a possible last name, is he really saying there is a third name as well? I think so.

So far, we have:

My Last name is Klein.
I am a Jewish man, born in 1924
In the Navy, I am Kay

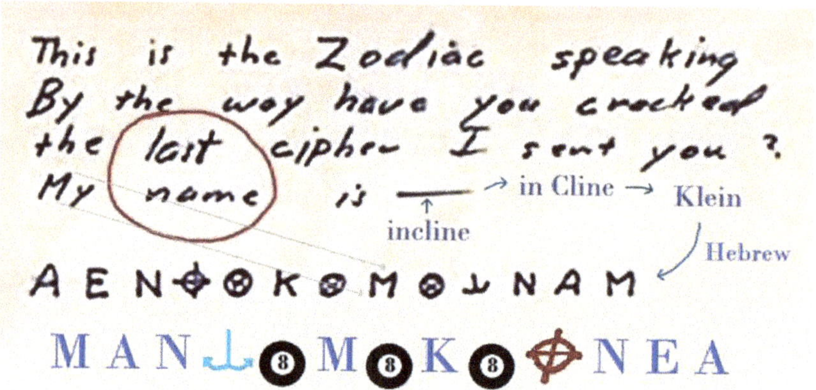

We finally arrive at the Zodiac sign ⊕, followed by "N E A" as if to say: "After I started killing people, I added "N E A" to my name." His name at that point would most likely be Kay, so he probably added "N E A" to "K". If I write "M" and "K" again, and use it for the third time since it's surrounded by 3 circled ⑧'s, and then line up the other 4 remaining characters of the code:

M K⊕NEA

It would read "I am KAYNEA" with the Zodiac in it. That doesn't really flow like the rest of the cipher, so here we would have to go back to his own line of thinking. Don't forget, in his mind, he is the endgame; he is the Zodiac, so what if we simply put ⊕ at the end of the game and end the game? What I did here is swap the last character "A" with the Zodiac symbol ⊕, making him at the end of this game. Now it lines up like this.

M KANE⊕

Or it reads:

I'm Kane as The Zodiac!

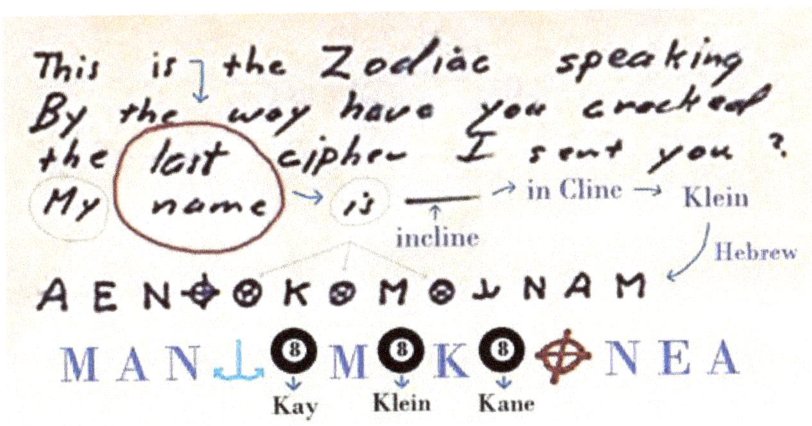

By this point, we realize that each circled ⑧ can represent one period in his life, as well as one last name he had in that period.

1. I am KLEIN when I was born in '24 ⑧
2. I am KAY when I was in the Navy ⑧
3. I am KANE as the Zodiac Killer ⑧

If we extract "My last name" from the opening message, and we see 3 ⑧'s as some sort of center piece of the code, I do believe that The Zodiac wanted to say: "If you find my 3 last names, you will find who I am."

To conclude this whole thing and glue it all together we are going to go back to the beginning of the message where he goes "This is the Zodiac Speaking," but if we go down from "This is," straight down to the code, it would read "This is the last name –> code," or that whole left side of the message almost reads as "This is, by the way, my last name cipher," either way with the "last name" connection, he laid a path that this is most likely.

"The Last Name Cipher"

Once we apply that to the entire code, we read!

My last name is KLEIN
I'm a Jewish man, born in 1924
In the Navy, my last name is KAY
My last name is KANE, as the Zodiac

Now the question is, does that person exist?

Larry Kane
"Man about Town"

Life-long criminal, born as Lawrence Klein in 1924, Brooklyn, New York, into a Jewish family. When he was about 17, he changed his name to Kaye. As we can see in this photo, "Employee's request for change in records."

Larry Kaye, born as Larry Klein in 1924

Reason for filing this request, he wrote: "Beneficial for employment in my field."

The entertainment field, master of ceremonies - M.C. is what he was reported to be. In control of the stage? Already in his early years, he seemed to enjoy managing the flow of the event, setting the stage, and engaging the audience.

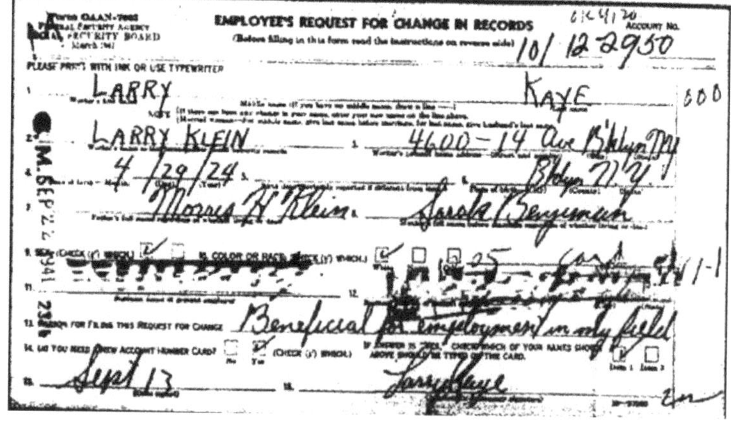

The Zodiac was the one running the show. He chose when to appear and when to disappear. He was the one building and designing the stage, and engaging the audience.

Another clue that can be found in the Zodiac letters is when he made the reference to "The Mikado" opera performance on more than one occasion. The first one was mailed on July 26, 1970. A new production of "The Mikado" opened on October 18, 1969, at the Presentation Theatre, San Francisco. We can notice on the actual poster of that performance that the set was designed and built by Larry Klein! Although we can be certain the actual Larry Klein who designed the stage for "The Mikado" is not Larry Kane, the Zodiac killer. However, more than likely, Kane saw the program for the show and figured that it would be a brilliant idea to point in the direction of the opera, presenting another hint where his name could be found, an in-your-face type of clue.

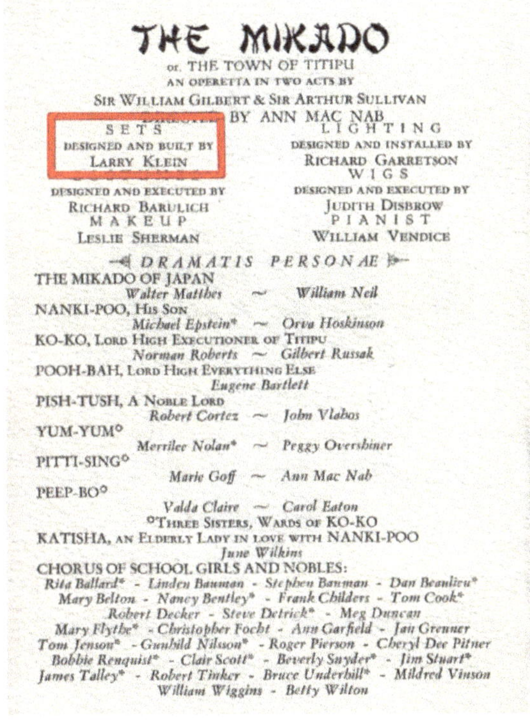

This letter he mailed to Miss. Eileen Barton Hotel Van Cortland, N.Y., from his naval base in Chicago

"L. Kaye Naval Armory Chicago"

The date is June 7, 1943, time of the ongoing World War II. He was 19 years old, and there he is in the navy uniform. Eileen Barton went on to become a well-known American Singer, performing with Frank Sinatra.

In some of the later letters mailed by the Zodiac killer, we can find that 3 of them were signed with a citizen's signature. First one being a "concerned citizen", followed by a "good citizen", and then some years later, he signed with just "a citizen". The movie "Citizen Kane" was released in 1941, and over time became a masterpiece of American cinematography. An obvious hint from Larry Kane, a concerned citizen.

Kane's official certification of military service with his original name, Lawrence Klein. The service took place from February 1943 to September 1943. In this document, we can see that his service was terminated.

"Honorable discharge," most likely for poor behavior. In the report listed as "Psychoneurosis Hysteria."

I HAVE BEEN DULY INFORMED OF THE FINDINGS OF A BOARD OF

MEDICAL SURVEY THAT MY PRESENT CONDITION ___________________

PSYCHONEUROSIS, HYSTERIA

IS CONSIDERED NOT IN THE LINE OF DUTY IN THAT IT EXISTED

PRIOR TO MY ENLISTMENT IN THE UNITED STATES NAVAL SERVICE.

I DO ADMIT THAT THIS CONDITION DID EXIST PRIOR TO MY EN-

LISTMENT IN THE UNITED STATES NAVAL SERVICE AND THAT IT HAS

NOT BEEN AGGRAVATED BY MY SERVICE IN THE UNITED STATES NAVAL

SERVICE.

LAWRENCE KLEIN

UNITED STATES OF AMERICA

Certification of
Military Service

This certifies that	Lawrence Klein
	809 73 37
was a member of the	United States Navy Reserve
from	February 5th, 1943
to	September 28th, 1943
Service was terminated by	Honorable Discharge
Last Grade, Rank, or Rating	S2c
Active Service Dates	Same As Above

Date of Birth: 04/29/1924   Place of Birth: Brooklyn, NY

Problematic behavior certainly followed him wherever he moved on. This official FBI document demonstrates his periodic dealings with law enforcement. We can see him here as Larry Kaye, his real name Lawrence Klein, then Lawrence Kane, Larry Kaye again, and so on. Conspiracy and fraud, burglary, battery, grand larceny... almost anything you can think of. On one occasion, he is listed as Barton, probably took that name from Miss. Eileen Barton. At the very end, we finally see him appear in California as Lawrence Kane, 1961, Alameda, "Peeping in the windows."

Interesting evolution of his activities.

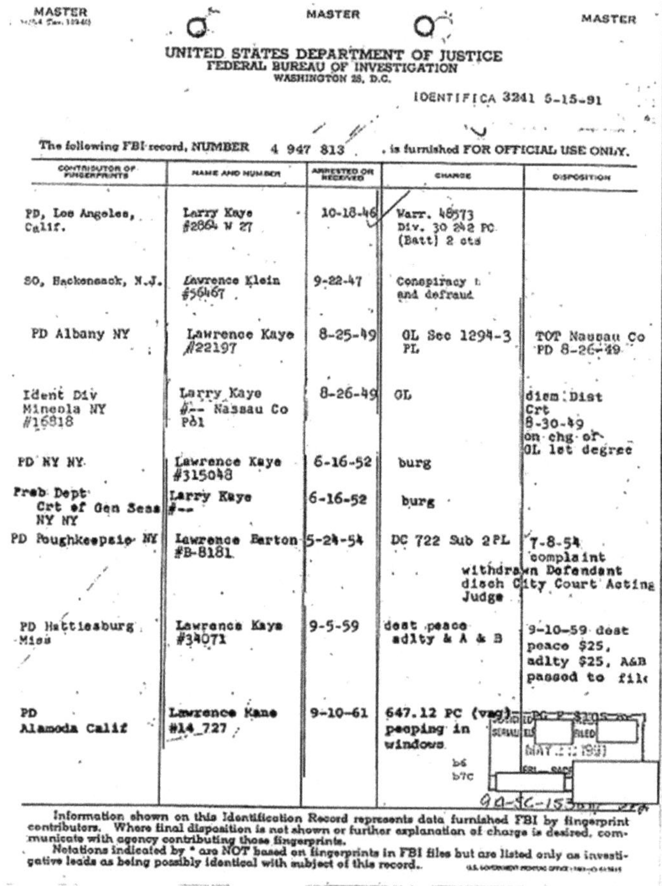

UNITED STATES DEPARTMENT OF JUSTICE
FEDERAL BUREAU OF INVESTIGATION
WASHINGTON 25, D.C.

IDENTIFICA 3241 5-15-91

The following FBI record, NUMBER 4 947 813 , is furnished FOR OFFICIAL USE ONLY.

CONTRIBUTOR OF FINGERPRINTS	NAME AND NUMBER	ARRESTED OR RECEIVED	CHARGE	DISPOSITION
PD, Los Angeles, Calif.	Larry Kaye #2864 W 27	10-18-46	Warr. 48573 Div. 30 242 PC (Batt) 2 cts	
SO, Hackensack, N.J.	Lawrence Klein #56467	9-22-47	Conspiracy t and defraud	
PD Albany NY	Lawrence Kaye #22197	8-25-49	OL Sec 1294-3 PL	TOT Nassau Co PD 8-26-49
Ident Div Mineola NY #16818	Larry Kaye #-- Nassau Co PO1	8-26-49	OL	diem Dist Crt 8-30-49 on chg of OL 1st degree
PD NY NY	Lawrence Kaye #315048	6-16-52	burg	
Prob Dept Crt of Gen Sess NY NY	Larry Kaye #--	6-16-52	burg	
PD Poughkeepsie NY	Lawrence Barton #B-8181	5-24-54	DC 722 Sub 2 PL	7-8-54 complaint withdrawn Defendant disch City Court Acting Judge
PD Hattiesburg Miss	Lawrence Kaye #34071	9-5-59	dest peace adlty & A & B	9-10-59 dest peace $25, adlty $25, A&B passed to file
PD Alameda Calif	Lawrence Kane #14_727	9-10-61	647.12 PC (vag) peeping in windows b6 b7c	

Information shown on this Identification Record represents data furnished FBI by fingerprint contributors. Where final disposition is not shown or further explanation of charge is desired, communicate with agency contributing those fingerprints.
Notations indicated by * are NOT based on fingerprints in FBI files but are listed only as investigative leads as being possibly identical with subject of this record.

On the next page of the same document, he can be seen as Larry Kane in Palo Alto, 1963, his real name in Menlo Park, 1965, again as Kane in Redwood City, 1968, most of these in the San Francisco area. Shoplifting, theft, credit card ill use, prowling ...

English meaning for prowling: To move around quietly in a place, trying not to be seen or heard, such as an animal does for hunting.

The first confirmed murder credited to the Zodiac was the double murder of high school students Betty Lou Jensen and David Faraday. The crime took place in the secluded Lover's Lane, on the night of December 20, 1968, in Vallejo, California. About 4 months after Kane was caught for quietly moving around, trying not to be seen or heard, such as an animal does for hunting.

MASTER
I-4 (Rev. 7-19-77)

2

UNITED STATES DEPARTMENT OF JUSTICE
FEDERAL BUREAU OF INVESTIGATION
IDENTIFICATION DIVISION
WASHINGTON, D. C. 20837

MASTER   MASTER

3241 5-15-91

Use of the following FBI record, NUMBER 4 947 813 , is REGULATED BY LAW. It is furnished FOR OFFICIAL USE ONLY and should ONLY BE USED FOR PURPOSE REQUESTED. When further explanation of arrest charge or disposition is needed, communicate directly with the agency that contributed the fingerprints.

CONTRIBUTOR OF FINGERPRINTS	NAME AND NUMBER	ARRESTED OR RECEIVED	CHARGE	DISPOSITION
PD Palo Alto CA	Larry Kane SCC 137664	12-3-63	PT shoplift	jail 30 das susp $50 F 1 yr informal prob
PD Oak Brook IL	Larry Kane 183	9-5-64	T (shplftg) 38-16-1	
SO Wheaton IL	Larry Kane 6178	9-5-64	theft	
PD Menlo Park CA	Lawerence Klein 577¼	3-27-65	484 PC PT	F 2 yrs prob formal
PD Miami Beach FL	Lawrence Kane A-47750	7-11-66	credit card (ill use)	Pd F of $50 & C
PD Redwood City CA	Lawrence Kane 24197	8-29-68	prowling	
SO Placerville CA	Larry Cane 49036 SID 1998641	10-1-80	T of personal prop	10das jl F $300 2yrs sw prob on chg of 484a PC

U.S. GOVERNMENT PRINTING OFFICE : 1980 O - 315-186

As we can see, these arrests alone place him in the area of the confirmed Zodiac murders, at the time the murders occurred. Kane's known address when the taxi driver was killed was 217 Eddy Street, San Francisco, about 2 blocks away from where Paul Stine picked up his passenger, his killer!

The building where Kane resided on Eddy Street would've been right in the heart of the San Francisco Theater District, the neighborhood where he would have easy access to spot the programs of the ongoing performances, including "The Mikado" show at that time.

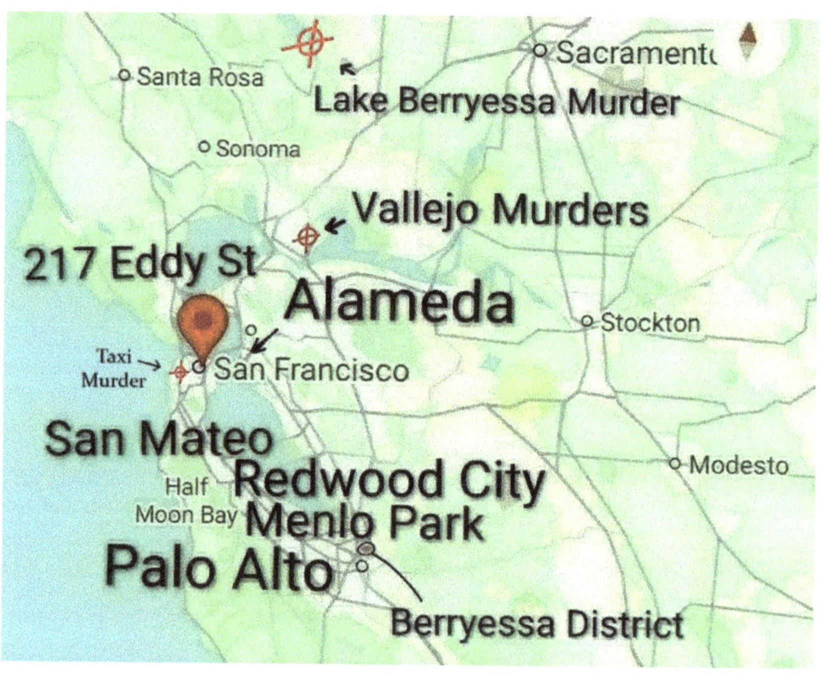

The murder in Vallejo in July 1969

Darlene Ferrin - murdered, Mike Mageau - wounded

Darlene was allegedly harassed by a man recognized as Kane during her shifts at the local restaurant.

The murder at Lake Berryessa in September 1969

Cecilia Shepard - murdered, Bryan Hartnell – wounded.

Was it a possible hint that Kane had some business in the Berryessa district of the Bay Area? Unknown…

Following his trail, we can clearly see how Kane goes from being the Master of Ceremony in New York, an entertainer acting and performing on stage, to dealing with mental problems while serving the navy in Chicago, back as a salesman in New York, a gangster who was getting arrested for theft, shoplifting, fraud & conspiracy, assault & battery, a realtor in San Francisco, a swindler who was getting involved with voyeurism, peeping in windows, prowling, adultery & disturbing the peace.

Salesman Held On Conduct Charge

Lawrence Barton, 30-year-old New York City Salesman, arrested here May 24 on a disorderly conduct charge also is known as Lawrence "Larry" Kaye, Police Chief Martin reported last night.

It is understood that Kaye once was accused of robbing the apartment of Mrs. Johnny Johnston, wife of singer Johnny Johnston.

Barton is free here in $50 bail and his case still is pending in City court.

Chief Martin said the City Police department learned Barton also is known as Kaye from an FBI report. It wasn't made known which is the defendant's real name and which is his assumed name, but it is believed that Kaye is his real name.

At 11:20 o'clock on the night of May 23, Police received a telephone call from the home of Dennis Crawford, 21 Gate street, that Mr. Crawford was holding a prowler in his yard at the point of a shotgun.

* * *

SERGEANT MANERI and Patrolmen Dugan and Berberick and Detective Morris were sent to the scene. They found Mr. Crawford holding an unloaded shotgun and pointing it at a man identified as Barton.

Barton was holding his shoes because he had corns on both feet. Mr. Crawford told City Judge McCoy he ordered Barton from his yard once and about 45 minutes later he found the defendant again in his yard and he held him at bay with the shotgun until police arrived.

Barton said he was staying at the Poughkeepsie Inn. He added that he was employed by a Smith street paint concern.

Gangster Drivers Face Damage Suit

HOLLYWOOD, Oct. 22 (UP)—Three New York motorists charged with beating up two pedestrians who bawled them out after a near-accident today faced a $40,000 damage suit.

James and Kathryn Drane said they were almost run down last October 15 while crossing Vine street. They said they shouted, "Why don't you be more careful?" — Only to have the car's occupants, Larry Kaye and Max Schulman, leap from the auto and assault them.

The defendants were arrested and released on $250 bail each pending trial.

FIANCEE OF SINGER ROBBED BY HIS PAL

By the United Press

NEW YORK—A burglar who participated in the theft of $17,000 in jewelry from the apartment of Mrs. Shirley Carmel was identified today as a friend of the victim's fiance, Singer Johnny Johnston.

Larry Kaye, 28-year-old unemployed salesman, gave himself up yesterday after learning the police were closing in on him. He brought $6,000 in gems with him to the station house.

Mrs. Carmel said her fiance introduced her to Kaye last Christmas. She said he had seen Kaye several times since then.

Mrs. Carmel's maid identified Kaye as one of the two men who told her "we're friends of Shirley and Johnny" when she surprised them in her mistress' bedroom last week.

Kaye, whom police described as a man-about-town who knows a great many people in show business, said his partner in crime was a stranger he met in an east-side bar. He surrendered when he learned that his flashy yellow convertible had been spotted near the scene of the crime.

NEW YORK CITY PAIR GETS BAIL IN SWINDLE CASE

Third Member Of Ring To Waive Extradition, Fowler Reveals

OTHERS ARE SOUGHT

Charged with running a swindle that left householders holding the bag for the cost of new sidnig on their homes, two New York City men, Lawrence Klein, alias Kaye, 23, 215 West Ninety-fourth Street, and Nathan Benjamin, alias Barton, 32, 2345 Broadway, were released on $1,000 bail at the County Jail, Hackensack, yesterday.

They had surrendered themselves to an indictment by the Grand Jury which charges they are among a group of six salesmen participating in the operation. A third man, Irving Troy, also of New York City, is reported by the Prosecutor's Office to have waived extradition and will be brought over today.

According to Martin K. Fowler, financial investigator for the Prosecutor's Office, the salesmen operated in Oradell, Maywod, River Edge an dother Bergen towns, by offering to put siding on a home if the owner would agree to let his home be used as a model to interest other prospects. The owner was to get $25 for each prospect, said Fowler.

In closing the deal the householder was asked to sign application for F. H. A. credit, a note, and a certificate of completion, who would discount the notes at a bank, he went on.

The pinch came when the home owner suddenly found that the note he signed was due at a bank, and that he had not received something for nothing, concluded Fowler.

On December 4, 1963, the Palo Alto Peninsula Times reports that Kane was apprehended and held for the police by a store detective at the shopping plaza. Allegedly stole the toy priced at 15.95$, while he had 1160$ in cash on him. In 1963, 1160$ would be roughly $12,000 in today's money. Here we can assume that Kane performed his crimes for the thrill of let's see if I can get away with this one, seeing himself on the opposite side of the Police Department.

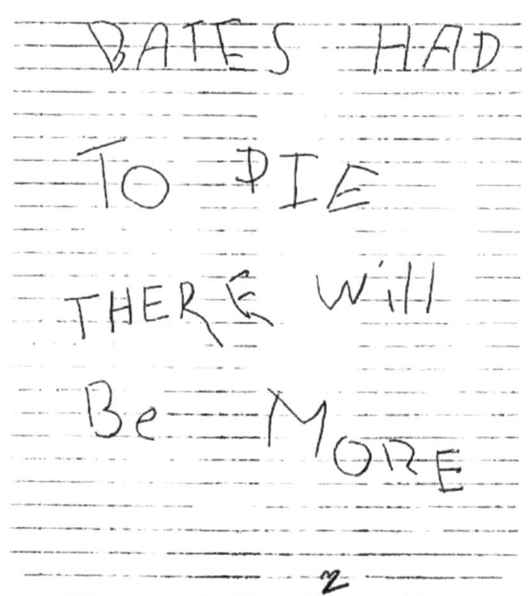

Man carrying $1,160 accused of stealing toy

A toy wheel of fortune spun out a tale of woe Tuesday night for a 39-year-old Burlingame man.

Palo Alto police said the man, Larry Kane of 1469 Bellview Drive, gambled and lost when he tucked a toy roulette wheel under his coat and tried to leave Norney's Toy Store in the Stanford Shopping Center without paying for it.

Kane was apprehended and held for police by J o s e p h S. Suske, 22, of San Francisco, a store detective at the Roos-Atkins store in the plaza. Suske told police he became suspicious after Kane entered Roos-Atkins several times and left each time without buying anything. He trailed Kane to the toy store.

Kane, who police said was carrying $1,160 in cash when he was arrested, was booked into the North County Jail on a charge of petty theft. The toy he allegedly stole was priced at $15.95. He was released after posting $276 bail and ordered to appear for arraignment Dec. 13.

"Bates had to die" was sent to the Riverside Police Department on April 30, 1967. Exactly 6 months after Cheri Jo Bates, a probable Zodiac victim, was found dead on the campus of Riverside City College, California. The note was signed with some type of "Z" signature, number 3 coming into the diagonal line, all together forming the letter Z. This seems like Kane was implying that his 3 different last names are coming into his signature, forming the Zodiac persona.

One and only homicide investigator who had Kane as the Zodiac suspect, Harvey Hines, pointed out that Kane stayed clear of the police from 1968 to 1979, when he was arrested for hooking up a telephone illegally, this time as Cane with C. Suddenly, something caused him to change in the late '60s and clean up his act? Or he simply perfected his criminal act and was able to avoid the attention of the police as the Zodiac.

Hard to believe that all those consistent criminal acts just magically stopped in 1968, 4 months before the double murder in Vallejo.

The Zodiac **Eyewitness description**	**Larry Kane** **1968-1969**
Race: white	Race: white
Age: 35-45	Age: 44-45
Height: 5'8-5'10	Height: 5'9
Weight: 180 – 210lbs	Weight: Approximately 175lbs
Build: heavy-set, stocky	Build: stocky, pot belly
Eyes: heavy rim eyeglasses	Eyes: wearing glasses
Face: large, round face	Face: round face
Hair: short curly hair, brown	Hair: short curly dark hair

The disappearance of Donna Lass on September 6, 1970, is more than likely tied to the Zodiac's postcard mailed on March 22, 1971. Using a slightly different method in this card, the Zodiac suggested to the investigators to try to find his 12th victim around in the snow, past Lake Tahoe areas, in the direction of the Sierra Club, which would roughly be 50 miles away from the abduction point. Was this cryptic message a little hint that the Zodiac moved on to the Lake Tahoe area? Well, Larry Kane moved to South Lake Tahoe in June 1970, a few months before Donna disappeared after her shift ended at the Sahara Tahoe Hotel and Casino. According to the investigation of H. Hines, Kane worked in the real estate office in the lobby of the same hotel, across the first aid station where Donna worked as a registered nurse. She lived 15 minutes' walk from the hotel, in Monte Verdi Apartments, on Pioneer Trail. Donna's remains were found years later near Discovery Trails of the Sierra Mountains, not too far from Donner Pass Road.

Indeed, the remains were located as suggested in the postcard, pass Lake Tahoe areas, in the direction of the Sierra Club Lodges, the Donner Pass area. The Donner Party is a well-known American group of pioneers who were stuck "around in the snow" in the Sierra Mountains.

Donner Pass - Donna Lass - Pioneer Trail, we clearly see how Kane liked to play with words and with human lives just to satisfy his perverted needs.

One unconfirmed Zodiac victim, Dana Lull, was abducted and murdered on April 27, 1974. She was taken at gunpoint while being with her boyfriend in a secluded lover's lane area near Las Vegas. The couple was in the boyfriend's car when the suspect approached them, wearing black gloves and holding an automatic pistol. The boyfriend, Roy Topigh, managed to escape before Dana and the suspect drove off in the kidnapper's car. Described by the boyfriend as a 1968 sports car convertible, white with a black roof. The suspect was described as 5'9, with a round face, short dark hair, and horn-rimmed glasses. Two weeks later, Dana's dead body was found 125 miles away from where she was abducted. The body was abandoned near Mojave National Preserve, on Mountain Springs Rd. Larry Kane's known address at the time was 2439 Spring Mountain Rd, Las Vegas. About 5 miles away from where the young couple just wanted to be left alone. Kane decided to drive 125 miles across the desert to the remote location just to leave a clue about his location, where the police can find him. Records from 1974 show that Kane owned a 1968 MGB convertible sports car, white with a black top. Another murder, another hint left by the Zodiac.

FBI Enters Case Of Missing Girl

A widening search of the desert around Red Rock Canyon has failed to turn up any sign of 15-year-old Dana Marie Lull, a student at Western High School who was kidnaped from her boyfriend's car in that area last weekend.

Roy Tophigh, 21, her companion, told police the girl was forced into another car at gunpoint by a stranger neither had seen before.

Police helicopters and search teams in jeeps have scoured the Redrock area as far as Mountain Springs Summit without finding a trace of the girl, her clothing or any clue to her disappearance.

Meanwhile it was reported the Federal Bureau of Investigation had entered the case. Miss Lull's photo, physical description and chain of events surrounding the kidnaping have been flashed to all law enforcement agencies in the Western states

Police said the only leads they had were a description furnished by Tophigh of the kidnaper and his car but not its license number. The auto is believed to be a low-slung Triumph Spitfire several years old, painted white with a black top. It is possibly a convertible, police said

The kidnaper is between 30 and 40, short and stocky who at the time was wearing a dark suit, tie, gloves and glasses.

From some people who knew him, we can be informed that Kane was "An egotist, very stuck on himself, secretive, and guarded in his dealings with other people, neighbors didn't know what he did, kept the windows blinds down continuously."

Looking at "The petition for change of name" from 1989, we see that petitioner Lawrence Klein desires to take a new name of Lawrence Cane, followed by the reason for such a change...

Most likely a pack of lies. In my opinion, he certainly wanted to dissociate himself from K in his last name and from that whole criminal past that came with the previous last names.

IN THE NINTH JUDICIAL DISTRICT COURT OF THE STATE OF NEVADA

IN AND FOR THE COUNTY OF DOUGLAS

In the Matter of the
Application of: PETITION FOR CHANGE OF NAME

        LAWRENCE KLEIN, aka
LARRY CANE
            Petitioner,

For Change of Name
_______________________________/

    The Petition of LAWRENCE KLEIN respectfully shows:

    1. That Petitioner LAWRENCE KLEIN is a resident of the County of Douglas, State of Nevada and is over 21 years of age.

    2. That your Petitioner LAWRENCE KLEIN was born in New York, New York, on the 29th day of April, 1924; that his present name is LAWRENCE KLEIN; that he desires to take another nanme thatn that which he now has; that the new name which he proposes to take and assume is LAWRENCE (LARRY) CANE; that the following are the reasons for such change of name: ever since early adulthood and for my entire life, I have used, as my true name, LAWRENCE (LARRY) CANE; that I am personally known by my friends, business associates by that name and for this reason only, I would like to change my name legally to this name.

We are looking at the individual who frequently changed his name, because he certainly had a lot to hide. Someone who frequently got in trouble with the law because he just couldn't stop himself from getting more and more perverted and deranged.

Someone who gradually developed a strong need to commit a baffling crime, taunt the police, provide them with more than enough clues, and still show them the middle finger remaining unidentified.

A person who was able to keep a secret and stay undetected until he died in 2010. Lawrence Cane is what's engraved on his gravestone, a World War II veteran who "Will never be forgotten."

Kane truly has to be remembered for who he really was. Prowling predator who thought it would be fun to combine murders and codes with mystery, leaving behind clues and fear that made him feel he was the one in control, running this twisted show. Life-long criminal with a deep-seated need to puzzle the police, turning into The Zodiac serial Killer.

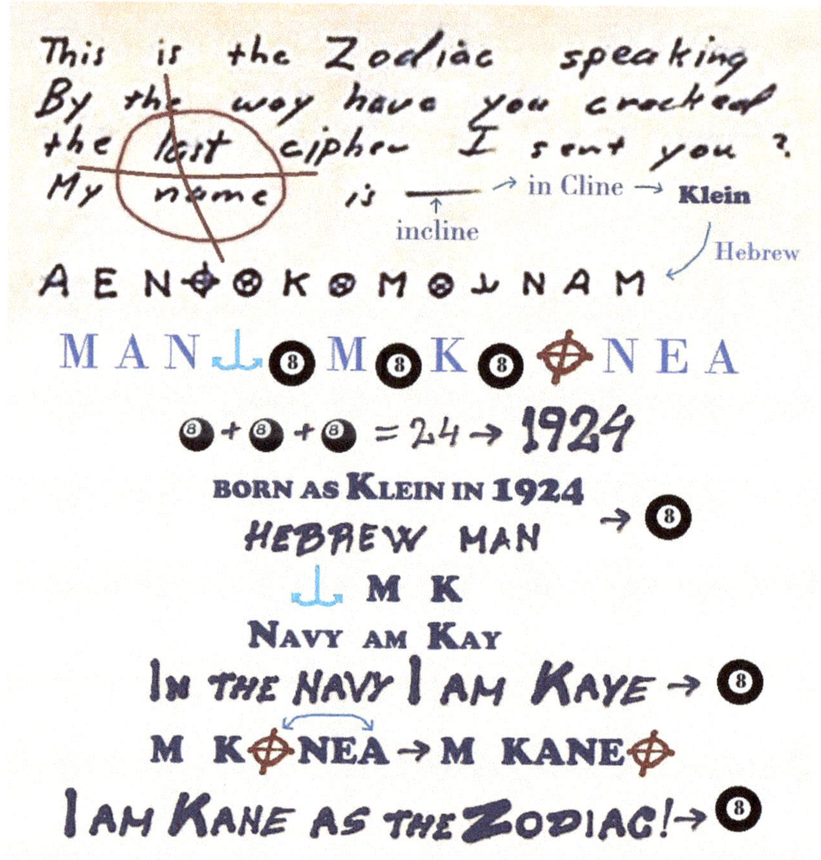

In "The Little List" letter, mailed on July 26, 1970, 3 months after he mailed "My Name Is" letter, the Zodiac mentioned a billiard game, more precisely billiard players. Describing what he will do to his "slaves", in one sentence, he stated: "And all billiard players I shall have them play in a darkened dungen cell with crooked cues + Twisted shoes." Not only did he provide a key to his last name cypher, he also meant to say: "Once I do my thing, all you people who are trying to find me, find my head (billiard players), I will have you in the dark basement room, unable to see anything, unable to see what's in front of your eyes (darkened dungen cell), unable to think straight, unable to aim straight (crooked cues), and unable to walk straight (+ Twisted shoes). You won't know where to look, what to think, and where to go!" The 8-ball was the key.

"This is the Zodiac speaking,
My last name is Klein
I am a Jewish Man, born in 1924
In the Navy, my last name was Kaye
My last name as the Zodiac Killer is Kane!"
April 20, 1970

The Zodiac was at the end of the game!

Contents